Great Is Thy
Faithfulness

© 2013 by Barbour Publishing, Inc.

Written and compiled by JoAnne Simmons.

Print ISBN 978-1-62029-805-3

eBook Editions:
Adobe Digital Edition (.epub) 978-1-62416-032-5
Kindle and MobiPocket Edition (.prc) 978-1-62416-031-8

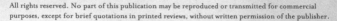

Scripture quotations marked KJV are taken from the King James Version of the Bible.

Scripture quotations marked NKJV are taken from the New King James Version®. Copyright © 1982 by Thomas Nelson, Inc. Used by permission. All rights reserved.

Scripture quotations marked NIV are taken from the HOLY BIBLE, NEW INTERNATIONAL VERSION®, NIV®. Copyright © 1973, 1978, 1984, 2011 by Biblica, Inc.™ Used by permission. All rights reserved worldwide.

Scripture quotations marked ESV are from The Holy Bible, English Standard Version®, copyright © 2001 by Crossway Bibles, a publishing ministry of Good News Publishers. Used by permission. All rights reserved.

Scripture quotations marked NLT are taken from the *Holy Bible*. New Living Translation copyright© 1996, 2004, 2007 by Tyndale House Foundation. Used by permission of Tyndale House Publishers, Inc. Carol Stream, Illinois 60188. All rights reserved.

Scripture quotations marked NASB are taken from the New American Standard Bible, © 1960, 1962, 1963, 1968, 1971, 1972, 1973, 1975, 1977, 1995 by The Lockman Foundation. Used by permission.

Published by Barbour Publishing, Inc., P.O. Box 719, Uhrichsville, Ohio 44683,
www.barbourbooks.com

Our mission is to publish and distribute inspirational products offering exceptional value and biblical encouragement to the masses.

Member of the
Evangelical Christian
Publishers Association

Printed in the United States of America.

Great Is Thy

Faithfulness

Inspiration from the Beloved Hymn

BARBOUR
PUBLISHING

Contents

Introduction: Great Is Thy Faithfulness ..6

God's Great Faithfulness 9

Faithful Father 21

Faithfully Unchanging..................... 33

Faithfully Compassionate.................. 45

Faithfully Amazing 57

Faithfully Merciful 69

Faithful Provider 83

Faithful Timekeeper 97

Faithful Creator 109

Faithful Savior and Peace 123

Faithful Companion...................... 135

Faithful Encourager and Guide 147

Faithful Strength 159

Faithful Hope 171

Faithfully Worthy 183

Great Is Thy Faithfulness

Great is Thy faithfulness, O God my Father;
There is no shadow of turning with Thee;
Thou changest not, Thy compassions, they fail not.
As Thou hast been, Thou forever wilt be.

Great is Thy faithfulness!
Great is Thy faithfulness!
Morning by morning new mercies I see.
All I have needed Thy hand hath provided;
Great is Thy faithfulness, Lord, unto me!

Summer and winter and springtime and harvest,
Sun, moon, and stars in their courses above
Join with all nature in manifold witness
To Thy great faithfulness, mercy, and love.

Pardon for sin and a peace that endureth
Thine own dear presence to cheer and to guide;
Strength for today and bright hope for tomorrow,
Blessings all mine, with ten thousand beside!

THOMAS O. CHISHOLM, 1923

God's Great Faithfulness

"Great Is Thy Faithfulness" is a beautiful, beloved hymn, and it is even more beautiful when we look deeper into its meaning.

The dictionary gives one meaning of *faithfulness* as "loyalty." In a fallen world, people unfortunately often fail at loyalty. Marriages fall apart; families feud among themselves; deep and lasting friendships are hard to come by. Since we humans mess it up so much, many people often think of a beloved pet dog—man's best friend—as the image of ultimate loyalty. But the God who said "I will never leave you nor forsake you" (Hebrews 13:5 ESV) is the only One truly unfaltering and untiring in His loyalty to His people.

Faithfulness is also defined as a "firm keeping of promises." We've all experienced the disappointment from a promise not kept. And no matter how good and strong our intentions,

we're all guilty of breaking promises to others, too. God, however, will never let us down with a broken promise. Deuteronomy 7:9 tells us, "Understand, therefore, that the LORD your God is indeed God. He is the faithful God who keeps his covenant for a thousand generations and lavishes his unfailing love on those who love him and obey his commands" (NLT).

Finally *faithfulness* is "worthiness of trust." Who is worthier of our trust than the God who created every detail about us (Psalm 139:13), has every hair on our heads numbered (Matthew 10:30), has good plans for us and our futures (Jeremiah 29:11), and who gave up His own Son to die that we might live (John 3:16–17)?

God abundantly fulfills every meaning of the word *faithful*. Yes, "*great* is Thy faithfulness"!

Thy mercy, O LORD, is in the heavens;
and thy faithfulness reacheth unto the clouds.

PSALM 36:5 KJV

I will sing of the steadfast love of the LORD, forever;
with my mouth I will make known your
faithfulness to all generations. For I said,
"Steadfast love will be built up forever;
in the heavens you will establish your faithfulness."

PSALM 89:1–2 ESV

God is faithful even
when his children are not.
MAX LUCADO

Because God is faithful. . .I will trust
Him to always keep His promises.
DR. WILLIAM R. BRIGHT

God's faithfulness means that
God will always do what He said and
fulfill what He has promised.
WAYNE GRUDEM

Know therefore that the LORD thy God, he is God, the faithful God, which keepeth covenant and mercy with them that love him and keep his commandments to a thousand generations.

DEUTERONOMY 7:9 KJV

O LORD, You are my God; I will exalt You, I will give thanks to Your name; for You have worked wonders, plans formed long ago, with perfect faithfulness.

ISAIAH 25:1 NASB

You Are Great, God!

Dear Father, You are great and worthy
of all my praise. Great is Your faithfulness
to me; I would be so lost without You.
Great is Your love for me; I would not know
real love without it. Great are Your
blessings and promises for me; I really don't
deserve them. Great is Your mercy on me;
You forgive me again and again. God,
I praise You and thank You with all
that I am for all that You are! Amen.

For the LORD your God is a merciful God;
he will not abandon or destroy you or forget the covenant
with your ancestors, which he confirmed to them by oath.

DEUTERONOMY 4:31 NIV

Praise the LORD, all nations! Extol him, all peoples!
For great is his steadfast love toward us, and the faithfulness
of the LORD endures forever. Praise the LORD!

PSALM 117 ESV

When we face difficulties, we sometimes forget God's past faithfulness. We see only the detours and the dangerous path. But look back and you will also see the joy of victory, the challenge of the climb, and the presence of your Traveling Companion who has promised never to leave you nor forsake you.

UNKNOWN

Let God's promises shine on your problems.

CORRIE TEN BOOM

*"And now the L*ORD *has fulfilled the promise he made,*
for I have become king in my father's place, and I now
*sit on the throne of Israel, just as the L*ORD *promised.*
I have built this Temple to honor the name
*of the L*ORD*, the God of Israel."*

1 KINGS 8:20 NLT

Those who know your name trust in you, for you,
*L*ORD*, have never forsaken those who seek you.*

PSALM 9:10 NIV

Not Worthy

Dear Father, I fail so often in my faithfulness
to others and to You. Like Jacob prayed in
Genesis 32, I am not worthy of even the least
of all the things You have done for me in
Your steadfast love and constant faithfulness.
Regardless, You continue to love and bless and
provide for me. I can't thank You enough.
Please forgive me for my lack of faithfulness
and help me to model Yours. Amen.

Trusting God completely means having
faith that He knows what is best for
your life. You expect Him to keep His
promises, help you with problems,
and do the impossible when necessary.

RICK WARREN

God never made a promise
that was too good to be true.

D. L. MOODY

Faithful Father

Life is impossible without a father, but not everyone has or knows their earthly father or ever had a good one. For those who have or had a good one, the word *father* might equate with things like big, warm bear hugs and a sense of strength and security. For those who don't or didn't, the word *father* might evoke sadness, bitterness, and tears—tragically, even fear.

For those blessed with a good earthly father, the connection to our heavenly Father is often not difficult. When the Bible talks about God being our *Abba* (a Hebrew word that is a more intimate word for *father*, like *daddy*), those people can quickly relate and think of God as Provider, Comforter, Teacher, and Friend.

But for those who have never experienced a healthy and loving paternal relationship, they have a choice: either build a wall of rejection or unbelief against God our heavenly Father,

likening Him to their sinful human father, or reach out to Abba and fall into His divine arms, letting His perfect love and faithfulness soothe their hurt and fulfill their needs.

Whether good or bad, no earthly father is perfect. Even the best are simply human and will fail us at times. But our God, to whom we can sing, "Great is Thy faithfulness, O God my Father," is absolutely perfect and absolutely faithful. His love and His care will never, ever let us down. "See what great love the Father has lavished on us, that we should be called children of God! And that is what we are!" (1 John 3:1 NIV).

But to all who believed him and accepted him, he gave the right to become children of God. They are reborn— not with a physical birth resulting from human passion or plan, but a birth that comes from God. So the Word became human and made his home among us. He was full of unfailing love and faithfulness. And we have seen his glory, the glory of the Father's one and only Son.

JOHN 1:12–14 NLT

I know of nothing which so stimulates my faith in my heavenly Father as to look back and reflect on His faithfulness to me in every crisis and every chilling circumstance of life. Over and over He has proved His care and concern for my welfare. Again and again I have been conscious of the Good Shepherd's guidance through dark days and deep valleys.

PHILLIP KELLER

*For the Father Himself loves you,
because you have loved Me and have
believed that I came forth from the Father.*

JOHN 16:27 NASB

*Now may our Lord Jesus Christ himself, and God
our Father, who loved us and gave us eternal comfort
and good hope through grace, comfort your hearts
and establish them in every good work and word.*

2 THESSALONIANS 2:16–17 ESV

Thanks for Good Fathers

Dear Father, thank You for being the best
Father, the only One who will never fail us.
And thank You for good men who follow You
and strive to model You as a father to their
children. The world needs more good fathers,
and I pray that You would raise them up as
leaders in their homes, in their communities,
in the church, and in our world. Thank
You for all the good earthly fathers You have
created and called to Your service. Amen.

"I will be a Father to you, and you shall be My sons and daughters, says the LORD Almighty."

2 CORINTHIANS 6:18 NKJV

He is the Rock, his works are perfect, and all his ways are just. A faithful God who does no wrong, upright and just is he.

DEUTERONOMY 32:4 NIV

But the Christian also knows that he not
only cannot and dare not be anxious, but that
there is no need for him to be so. Neither
anxiety nor work can secure his daily bread,
for bread is the gift of the Father.

DIETRICH BONHOEFFER

The beautiful thing about this
adventure called faith is that we can
count on Him never to lead us astray.

CHARLES SWINDOLL

*"God is not a man, so he does not lie. He is
not human, so he does not change his mind.
Has he ever spoken and failed to act? Has he
ever promised and not carried it through?"*

NUMBERS 23:19 NLT

*For he loves us with unfailing love;
the LORD's faithfulness endures forever.*

PSALM 117:2 NLT

Father of the Fatherless

Dear Father, there are so many in our
world without good fathers, whether
from death, neglect, broken families. . .
and the list goes on. But Your Word says
You are Father to the fatherless. Please hold
those who need a good father ever so close
to You. Comfort them with Your Word,
and love them through Your people. Show
them Your care and faithfulness, and help
them to trust You as a loving Daddy. Amen.

We forget that God sometimes has to say No.
We pray to Him as our heavenly Father,
and like wise human fathers, He often says, No,
not from whim or caprice, but from wisdom
and from love, and knowing what is best for us.

PETER MARSHALL

The purpose of rejoicing is not so we can feel
better emotionally (though that will happen).
The purpose of joy is to glorify God by
demonstrating to an unbelieving world that
our loving and faithful heavenly Father cares
for us and provides for us all that we need.

JERRY BRIDGES

Faithfully Unchanging

You only have to look at a baby's photos from month to month to see how quickly life can change. Unfortunately, not all changes are as sweet as those of a healthy baby's growth and development. Just read or listen to the news for plenty of examples. Many of life's changes are utterly devastating. And for some, even small changes cause major stress. For the most part, we like to settle deep down into our comfort zones with a satisfied *ahhhh* and pray for no disruptions. Unfortunately, the disruptions are inevitable. But in a world where it seems nothing much stays the same for more than a few minutes or months at most, isn't it good to know that there is an almighty God who is our one true constant?

As the song goes, "There is no shadow of turning with Thee; Thou changest not. . ." These words are a reference to the King James

Version of James 1:17, which says, "Every good gift and every perfect gift is from above, and cometh down from the Father of lights, with whom is no variableness, neither shadow of turning." An updated version reads, "Whatever is good and perfect comes down to us from God our Father, who created all the lights in the heavens. He never changes or casts a shifting shadow" (NLT).

The song and the scripture are making the point that God does not change. *Ever.* No matter how far out of our comfort zones change takes us, we can find lasting, permanent comfort in our unchanging heavenly Father.

God also bound himself with an oath, so that those who received the promise could be perfectly sure that he would never change his mind. So God has given both his promise and his oath. These two things are unchangeable because it is impossible for God to lie. Therefore, we who have fled to him for refuge can have great confidence as we hold to the hope that lies before us.

HEBREWS 6:17–18 NLT

A changeable God would be a terror to the
righteous, they would have no sure anchorage,
and amid a changing world they would
be driven to and fro in perpetual fear of
shipwreck. . . . Our heart leaps for joy as we
bow before One who has never broken His
word or changed His purpose.

CHARLES SPURGEON

Though our feelings come and go,
God's love for us does not.

C. S. LEWIS

"*For the mountains may depart and the hills be removed, but my steadfast love shall not depart from you, and my covenant of peace shall not be removed,*" *says the* L*ORD, who has compassion on you.*

ISAIAH 54:10 ESV

"*I the* L*ORD do not change. So you, the descendants of Jacob, are not destroyed.*"

MALACHI 3:6 NIV

My Steadfast Comforter

Dear Father, too much change often makes me
long for a safe comfort zone. Please help me to
remember that no matter what, You alone are
my steadfast Comforter. The only true comfort
zone is in the center of Your will, where Your
sovereign, loving arms will protect and guide
me. Thank You for never leaving or forsaking
me. Thank You for never changing. Amen.

*For the word of the L*ORD *is upright, and all His work
is done in faithfulness. He loves righteousness and justice;
the earth is full of the lovingkindness of the L*ORD.

PSALM 33:4–5 NASB

*Oh, how I love your instructions! I think about them
all day long. Your commands make me wiser than
my enemies, for they are my constant guide.*

PSALM 119:97–98 NLT

Consider what you owe to His immutability.
Though you have changed a thousand times,
He has not changed once.

CHARLES SPURGEON

Whatever apostasy occurs in Christianity,
it may never prompt us to question the
unchanging faithfulness of God, the certainty
of His counsel, the enduring character of
His covenant, or the trustworthiness of His
promises. One should sooner abandon all
creatures than fail to trust His Word.

HERMAN BAVINCK

*"The Glory of Israel will not lie or change His mind;
for He is not a man that He should change His mind."*
1 Samuel 15:29 nasb

*But the LORD's plans stand firm forever;
his intentions can never be shaken.*
Psalm 33:11 nlt

*Jesus Christ is the same yesterday
and today and forever.*
Hebrews 13:8 nasb

Thank You for Change

Dear Father, I'll be honest that in my selfishness, I only want good changes in my life. But I need to thank You for all change in my life, both good and bad, because You use change to mature me and draw me closer to You. You've shown me in the past and Your Word promises me that You will work all things for good for those who love You. Please help me to remember that promise. Amen.

Feelings come and feelings go,
And feelings are deceiving;
My warrant is the Word of God—
Naught else is worth believing.

Though all my heart should feel condemned
For want of some sweet token,
There is One greater than my heart
Whose Word cannot be broken.

I'll trust in God's unchanging Word
Till soul and body sever,
For, though all things shall pass away,
HIS WORD SHALL STAND FOREVER!

MARTIN LUTHER

Faithfully Compassionate

Henry Ward Beecher once said, "God pardons like a mother, who kisses the offense into everlasting forgiveness." Our God is our heavenly Father, but His compassion for us is perhaps best exhibited in the way He created mothers to care for and love their children. A good mother has endless, unconditional love and compassion for her children, and no amount of anger or mistakes will ever change that. Ask any mother who has held her arms open to a child with fat tears spilling from his sorrowful eyes, hiccupping out, "I'm sorry!" Or ask the mother who has helped hold down a child during a painful medical procedure or stood beside her child's hospital bed, praying desperately that she might take the pain herself instead.

As hard as it is to imagine, God's love and compassion for us is even better than a devoted

mother. Like the song says, "Thy compassions they fail not"—they cannot fail because He *is* love. No matter what we do, no matter how angry and hurt our *sin* might make Him, He still loves *us*, His children. In Isaiah He asks, "Can a woman forget her nursing child, and not have compassion on the son of her womb? Surely they may forget, yet I will not forget you" (49:15 NKJV). A mother's compassions rarely fail; God's compassions *never* fail.

*The LORD passed in front of Moses, calling out, "Yahweh!
The LORD! The God of compassion and mercy! I am slow to
anger and filled with unfailing love and faithfulness."*

EXODUS 34:6 NLT

*But you, Lord, are a compassionate and gracious God,
slow to anger, abounding in love and faithfulness.*

PSALM 86:15 NIV

The LORD is gracious and full of compassion.

PSALM 111:4 KJV

A teardrop on earth summons
the King of heaven.

CHARLES SWINDOLL

God is not proud. He will have us
even though we have shown that
we prefer everything else to Him.

C. S. LEWIS

Remember that even Jesus' most scathing
denunciation—a blistering diatribe against the
religious leaders of Jerusalem in Matthew 23
—ends with Christ weeping over Jerusalem.
Compassion colored everything He did.

JOHN MACARTHUR

So the LORD must wait for you to come to him so he can show you his love and compassion. For the LORD is a faithful God. Blessed are those who wait for his help.

ISAIAH 30:18 NLT

Then I will punish their transgression with the rod and their iniquity with stripes, but I will not remove from him my steadfast love or be false to my faithfulness.

PSALM 89:32–33 ESV

Open Arms

Dear Father, I'm so grateful that Your
compassion will never fail me, even when I
least deserve it. With my sin I make such a mess
sometimes, but no matter how ugly the sins,
You never reject me. Like a dear mother's
arms, Your arms are also always open and
waiting for me, ready to comfort and reassure
me that You'll never stop loving me. I can't
thank You enough. Amen.

The LORD's lovingkindnesses indeed never cease,
For His compassions never fail. They are new every
morning; Great is Your faithfulness. "The LORD is my
portion," says my soul, "Therefore I have hope in Him."
LAMENTATIONS 3:22–24 NASB

But He, being full of compassion, forgave their iniquity,
and did not destroy them. Yes, many a time He turned
His anger away, and did not stir up all His wrath;
For He remembered that they were but flesh.
PSALM 78:38–39 NKJV

No matter how low down you are; no matter
what your disposition has been; you may
be low in your thoughts, words, and actions;
you may be selfish; your heart may be
overflowing with corruption and wickedness;
yet Jesus will have compassion upon you.
He will speak comforting words to you;
not treat you coldly or spurn you, as perhaps
those of earth would, but will speak tender words,
and words of love and affection and kindness.
Just come at once. He is a faithful friend—
a friend that sticketh closer than a brother.

D. L. MOODY

*Who is a God like You, who pardons iniquity and passes
over the rebellious act of the remnant of His possession?
He does not retain His anger forever, because He delights
in unchanging love. He will again have compassion on us;
He will tread our iniquities under foot. Yes, You will
cast all their sins into the depths of the sea.*

MICAH 7:18–19 NASB

God with Us

Dear Father, Your Word says You sent
Your Son, Jesus, to be made like us in
every way so that He might be merciful to
us, take away our sins, and help us in our
temptations. You sent Your Son to be
"Immanuel, God with us" and to relate to us
in every detail of our lives. May I never forget
that there is no greater compassion than Your
giving up Your own Son for me. Amen.

As I look back over fifty years of ministry,
I recall innumerable tests, trials, and
times of crushing pain. But through it all,
the Lord has proven faithful, loving,
and totally true to all his promises.

DAVID WILKERSON

Someday we will celebrate Christ's
unwillingness to give in to our demands—
even when our begging broke His heart.
He is working the greater work. Still,
He has overwhelming compassion for
our pain and confusion.

BETH MOORE

Faithfully Amazing

"As Thou hast been, Thou forever wilt be. . . ." As complex and capable as our human brains might be, we can't possibly fully wrap them around the fact that God is eternal. There was no starting point of God. His Old Testament name is *Yahweh*, which is a Hebrew word for "I AM." He revealed Himself to Moses in the burning bush, saying, " 'I AM WHO I AM.' And he said, 'Say this to the people of Israel, I AM has sent me to you'" (Exodus 3:14 ESV). God simply *is*! He always has been, and He has no end.

Psalm 90:2 (ESV) describes God this way: "Before the mountains were brought forth, or ever you had formed the earth and the world, from everlasting to everlasting you are God."

Other attributes of God include His immutability, meaning He never changes (Malachi 3:6). God is omnipresent; He is everywhere all the time (Psalm 139:7–10). God

is omniscient; He knows everything (Psalm 33:13–15). God is omnipotent; He can do anything and has unlimited power (Genesis 18:14; Jeremiah 32:17).

How can we *not* trust such an awesome God? There is great power and comfort in knowing that the one, true God is bigger and better than all of our human ways and understanding. Because of His divine, supernatural attributes and abilities, He is the only One worthy of our complete trust. He is the only One *capable* of being perfectly faithful to us!

For the LORD is good and his love endures forever;
his faithfulness continues through all generations.

PSALM 100:5 NIV

Now to the King eternal, immortal, invisible, the only
God, be honor and glory forever and ever. Amen.

1 TIMOTHY 1:17 NASB

Everything about God is great, vast,
incomparable. He never forgets, never fails,
never falters, never forfeits His word.
To every declaration of promise or prophecy
the Lord has exactly adhered, every engagement
of covenant or threatening He will make good.

A. W. PINK

Never be afraid to trust an
unknown future to a known God.

CORRIE TEN BOOM

Great is our Lord and abundant in strength;
His understanding is infinite.

PSALM 147:5 NASB

LORD, you are my God; I will exalt you and praise
your name, for in perfect faithfulness you have
done wonderful things, things planned long ago.

ISAIAH 25:1 NIV

Mindful of Me

Dear Father, just like the psalmist who said, "What is man that you are mindful of him?" I, too, often wonder why You are mindful of me when You are such a great, almighty God and I am just one human among billions! Yet You know not just my name but even the number of hairs on my head. Wow. My brain can't really process how that's possible, so I will just have faith that it's true, and I praise You for it! Amen.

The eternal God is thy refuge,
and underneath are the everlasting arms:
and he shall thrust out the enemy from before thee.
DEUTERONOMY 33:27 KJV

Give thanks to the LORD, for he is good!
His faithful love endures forever.
1 CHRONICLES 16:34 NLT

A man can no more diminish God's glory
by refusing to worship Him than a lunatic
can put out the sun by scribbling the word
"darkness" on the walls of his cell.

C. S. LEWIS

The promises of the Bible are nothing
more than God's covenant to be faithful
to His people. It is His character that
makes these promises valid.

JERRY BRIDGES

Your word, Lord, is eternal; it stands firm in the heavens.
Your faithfulness continues through all generations;
you established the earth, and it endures.

Psalm 119:89–90 niv

Trust in the Lord forever, for the
Lord God is an everlasting rock.

Isaiah 26:4 esv

Indescribable

Dear Father, You are everywhere I am.
You know everything I think and do. You know
my worries, my cares, my dreams. You have
unlimited power to protect and provide for
me. And every individual person on this planet
can say the same. You are almighty God of each
and every one of us. Your attributes are utterly
indescribable. You are amazing, God, and I
am so grateful to be Your child. Amen.

An infinite God can give all of Himself
to each of His children. He does not
distribute Himself that each may have a part,
but to each one He gives all of Himself
as fully as if there were no others.

A. W. Tozer

We may ignore, but we can nowhere
evade, the presence of God.

C. S. Lewis

Faithfully Merciful

It's oh so easy to get stuck in a rut of a sinful attitude or behavior. Even the apostle Paul said, "I don't really understand myself, for I want to do what is right, but I don't do it. Instead, I do what I hate" (Romans 7:15 NLT). At the end of a long, rotten day full of our failures, sometimes the best we can do is cry out to God for help and try to muddle through until we make it to a new day.

What is it about a night of rest and waking up to another sunrise that can help us forget the mistakes of yesterday and start over again feeling forgiven and fresh? Maybe it's the fact that scripture says God's mercies are new every morning (Lamentation 3:22–23). Aren't you grateful you can sing, "Morning by morning new mercies I see," and know that it's true? Think how awful life would be if we had a heavenly Father who held our sins over our

heads or kept endless grudges or pinned guilt trips on us—how depressing and defeating that would be! But no, our loving Father faithfully offers us new mercy every single day, forgetting our faults immediately when we admit them and ask His forgiveness.

Mercy is often described as God not giving us the punishment we really deserve. We sure do mess things up sometimes, but we are incredibly blessed to have a loving Father who forgives, forgets, and faithfully grants us mercy.

*The steadfast love of the L*ORD *never ceases;*
his mercies never come to an end; they are
new every morning; great is your faithfulness.

LAMENTATIONS 3:22–23 ESV

If we confess our sins, he is faithful and
just and will forgive us our sins and
purify us from all unrighteousness.

I JOHN 1:9 NIV

Endless Mercy

Dear Father, I get so frustrated with myself
for doing what I know is wrong or struggling with
the same problem over and over again. Thank
You for loving me anyway. Where would I be
without Your endless mercy on me? Thank You
that *every single time* I ask for Your forgiveness, You
remove the sin from me as far as the east is from
the west. Thank You, Savior, *thank You*! Amen.

LORD, hear my prayer, listen to my cry for mercy;
in your faithfulness and righteousness come to my relief.

PSALM 143:1 NIV

As for you, O LORD, you will not restrain
your mercy from me; your steadfast love and
your faithfulness will ever preserve me!

PSALM 40:11 ESV

We fail Him, but, blessed be His name,
He has never failed us, and He never will do so.
We doubt Him, we mistrust His love and His
providence and His guidance; we "faint because
of the way"; we murmur because of the way;
yet all the time He is there blessing us and
waiting to pour out upon us a blessing so great
that there shall not be room to receive it.

UNKNOWN

It's Satan's delight to tell me that once he's got
me, he will keep me. But at that moment I can
go back to God. And I know that if I confess my
sins, God is faithful and just to forgive me.

ALAN REDPATH

Be ye therefore merciful,
as your Father also is merciful.

LUKE 6:36 KJV

Repent therefore and be converted, that
your sins may be blotted out, so that times of
refreshing may come from the presence of the Lord.

ACTS 3:19 NKJV

I Can Forgive

Dear Father, I need help in being as merciful to others as You are to me. It's so hard to let go of an offense sometimes. I don't want to quickly forget a wrong that's been done to me—I want the offender to hurt like I do. But I know that's not the right attitude. Help me to realize that with Your power working in me, I *can* forgive others, too, and the peace and freedom that will result is so much better than being slave to a grudge. Amen.

*Praise be to the God and Father of our Lord
Jesus Christ, the Father of compassion and the God
of all comfort, who comforts us in all our troubles.*

2 Corinthians 1:3–4 niv

*All of us used to live that way, following the passionate
desires and inclinations of our sinful nature. By our very
nature we were subject to God's anger, just like everyone
else. But God is so rich in mercy, and he loved us so much,
that even though we were dead because of our sins,
he gave us life when he raised Christ from the dead.*

Ephesians 2:3–5 nlt

The Gospel is good news of mercy to the undeserving. The symbol of the religion of Jesus is the cross, not the scales.

JOHN STOTT

God's mercy to us is the motivation for showing mercy to others. Remember, you will never be asked to forgive someone else more than God has forgiven you.

RICK WARREN

Let us then with confidence draw near to the
throne of grace, that we may receive mercy
and find grace to help in time of need.

HEBREWS 4:16 ESV

"For I will be merciful to their unrighteousness, and their
sins and their lawless deeds I will remember no more."

HEBREWS 8:12 NKJV

A Good Testimony

Dear Father, sometimes I wonder how You
can possibly make anything good result from
the messes I make in my work, in my home,
in my relationships with others. . . . But with
Your grace and mercy, even my worst actions
and attitudes can be turned around to bring
glory to You. Help me to be repentant and seek
Your forgiveness when I do wrong, and then
give me confidence that You will help me make
things right. Help me to be a good testimony
of Your faithful mercy. Amen.

When God is involved, anything can
happen. Be open. Stay that way.
God has a beautiful way of bringing
good vibrations out of broken chords.

CHARLES SWINDOLL

If God can make a billion galaxies, can't he
make good out of our bad and sense out of our
faltering lives? Of course he can. He is God.

MAX LUCADO

Sometimes God allows what he
hates to accomplish what he loves.

JONI EARECKSON TADA

Faithful Provider

Life certainly has its up and downs, times of plenty and times of not so much, but no matter our present circumstances, we can constantly sing, "All I have needed Thy hand hath provided." The God who knows when each sparrow falls considers His children worth far more than just the birds (Matthew 10:28–31), and He promises to love and provide for us. Jesus specifically told us not to worry about food or drink or clothes, for our heavenly Father knows that we need these things. We simply seek Him and His righteousness first, and all these things will be given to us as well (Matthew 6:25–34).

Unfortunately, our culture and our selfish nature make it hard to be content with having only our basic needs met. We want it all, and we want it now! But the closer we draw to God, the less we desire the things of this world—the

things that moth and rust destroy—and the more we long for our heavenly eternal home and the treasures there that moth and rust cannot destroy (Matthew 6:19–21).

There's a joke that you'll never see a U-Haul attached to a hearse, and its point is true! So we must choose to focus less on material items that we can't take to eternity and more on the things that do matter forever— our relationship with God, our relationships with others, and our good works that will store treasure for us in heaven, like loving, giving, serving, and sharing the Gospel (1 Timothy 6:17–19).

When we seek after God wholeheartedly, only then will we fully realize how true it is that *everything* we truly need, "Thy hand hath provided."

He provides food for those who fear him;
he remembers his covenant forever.

PSALM III:5 NIV

You sent abundant rain, O God, to refresh the weary land.
There your people finally settled, and with a bountiful
harvest, O God, you provided for your needy people.

PSALM 68:9–10 NLT

More of You

Dear Father, when I choose to focus on counting the blessings You've already given rather than the things I wish I had, I am overwhelmed with all You've given me. Draw me closer and closer to You so that I want more of You and less of the world. Help me to long for heaven and the treasures You are keeping for me there. I am blessed beyond measure. Thank You for faithfully providing for me. Amen.

*"Praise the LORD, who has given rest to his people Israel,
just as he promised. Not one word has failed of all the
wonderful promises he gave through his servant Moses."*
1 KINGS 8:56 NLT

*And my God will supply all your needs
according to His riches in glory in Christ Jesus.*
PHILIPPIANS 4:19 NASB

God's work done in God's way
will never lack God's supply.

HUDSON TAYLOR

Have you been holding back from a risky, costly
course to which you know in your heart God has
called you? Hold back no longer. Your God is
faithful to you, and adequate for you. You will
never need more than He can supply, and what
He supplies, both materially and spiritually,
will always be enough for the present.

J. I. PACKER

And God is able to bless you abundantly, so that in all things at all times, having all that you need, you will abound in every good work. As it is written: "They have freely scattered their gifts to the poor; their righteousness endures forever." Now he who supplies seed to the sower and bread for food will also supply and increase your store of seed and will enlarge the harvest of your righteousness. You will be enriched in every way so that you can be generous on every occasion, and through us your generosity will result in thanksgiving to God.

2 Corinthians 9:8–11 NIV

Cheerful Giver

Dear Father, please help me to be a cheerful giver. When I'm holding too tightly to my money and possessions, remind me that everything comes from You. When I think the numbers won't balance to give even a dollar away, remind me that You are not confined to a budget. You will provide everything I need plus more when I choose to give in love and in faith. Amen.

Simon Peter said, "I'm going fishing." "We'll come,
too," they all said. So they went out in the boat,
but they caught nothing all night. At dawn Jesus was
standing on the beach, but the disciples couldn't see who
he was. He called out, "Fellows, have you caught any
fish?" "No," they replied. Then he said, "Throw out
your net on the right-hand side of the boat, and you'll
get some!" So they did, and they couldn't haul in
the net because there were so many fish in it.

JOHN 21:3–6 NLT

God is ready to assume full responsibility
for the life wholly yielded to Him.

ANDREW MURRAY

Let us remember the loving-kindness of
the Lord and rehearse His deeds of grace.
Let us open the volume of recollection,
which is so richly illuminated with memories
of His mercy, and we will soon be happy.

ALISTAIR BEGG

Our need is not to prove God's faithfulness
but to demonstrate our own, by trusting
Him both to determine and to supply
our needs according to His will.

JOHN MACARTHUR

"You parents—if your children ask for a loaf of bread, do you give them a stone instead? Or if they ask for a fish, do you give them a snake? Of course not! So if you sinful people know how to give good gifts to your children, how much more will your heavenly Father give good gifts to those who ask him."

MATTHEW 7:9–11 NLT

I was young and now I am old, yet I have never seen the righteous forsaken or their children begging bread.

PSALM 37:25 NIV

Counting Blessings

Dear Father, my prayers are often that You provide financially, but money isn't everything. I need to be reminded constantly that Your best blessings don't come in the form of dollars and cents. You provide in so many other ways. Help me to daily count my blessings—and not just in a cliché way. I need to take time to quiet my heart and gratefully ponder all the things You've given and praise You for them. The list goes on and on and on. Amen.

Oftentimes God demonstrates His faithfulness in adversity by providing for us what we need to survive. He does not change our painful circumstances. He sustains us through them.

CHARLES STANLEY

Thankfulness to God is a recognition that God in His goodness and faithfulness has provided for us and cared for us, both physically and spiritually. It is a recognition that we are totally dependent upon Him; that all that we are and have comes from God.

JERRY BRIDGES

Faithful Timekeeper

"Summer and winter and springtime and harvest. . ." Singing about the seasons reminds us of the passing of time, and the older we get, the faster it flies. Just like the seasons of the year, there are seasons of life—sometimes difficult like a frigid, dark winter, sometimes pleasant like a not-too-hot summer. No season is perfect, but with the right attitude, we can find joy in them all. We might dread the signs of cooler weather coming and the endless leaf raking, but we can choose to delight in the colors of fall. We might detest the rains and mud of spring but can be grateful that they bring new life and growth.

There is bitter and sweet in every season of life, but we need to learn to accept them all, confident that God controls everything. Psalm 31:15 (NIV) says, "My times are in your hands." Our heavenly Father is our faithful timekeeper.

Every moment, every day, every season, every year—they are all kept and watched over by our Sovereign God. All our days and moments have been recorded by Him, from even before we were born (Psalm 139:16).

None of us can possibly know exactly how much time we'll have on this earth, but we can trust our God to keep track. We can choose to live whatever length of life we're given to His glory, seeking out the joy that is always there amid the pain, knowing our faithful timekeeper loves us and has good plans for us—and, even better, is preparing a timeless eternity for us.

My frame was not hidden from you when I was made in the secret place, when I was woven together in the depths of the earth. Your eyes saw my unformed body; all the days ordained for me were written in your book before one of them came to be.

PSALM 139:15–16 NIV

So teach us to number our days that we may get a heart of wisdom.

PSALM 90:12 ESV

Sovereign Schedule

Dear Father, in such an uncertain world,
it's so comforting to know that You are keeping
time. Since long before Creation, You've had
a sovereign schedule in place. It's not my job
to know or understand it, but I can choose to
believe it is best. You sent Your Son to save us
according to Your timing, and You will send
Him again at just the right time. You gave me
life according to Your timing, and You will take
me to eternity at just the right time. Meanwhile,
help me to live my life honoring You with each
moment You've given me. Amen.

Do not boast about tomorrow, for you
do not know what a day may bring forth.

PROVERBS 27:1 NASB

Look here, you who say, "Today or tomorrow we
are going to a certain town and will stay there a year.
We will do business there and make a profit." How do
you know what your life will be like tomorrow? Your
life is like the morning fog—it's here a little while,
then it's gone. What you ought to say is, "If the Lord
wants us to, we will live and do this or that."

JAMES 4:13–15 NLT

"All the paths of the Lord are loving and
faithful" (Psalm 25:10). I have pondered
this verse lately, and have found that it feeds
my spirit. All does not mean "all—except the
paths I am walking in now," or "nearly all—
except this especially difficult and painful
path." All must mean all. So, your path with
its unexplained sorrow or turmoil, and mine
with its sharp flints and briers—and both
our paths, with their unexplained perplexity,
their sheer mystery—they are His paths,
on which he will show himself loving and
faithful. Nothing else; nothing less.

AMY CARMICHAEL

Therefore we do not lose heart. Though outwardly we are wasting away, yet inwardly we are being renewed day by day. For our light and momentary troubles are achieving for us an eternal glory that far outweighs them all. So we fix our eyes not on what is seen, but on what is unseen, since what is seen is temporary, but what is unseen is eternal.

2 CORINTHIANS 4:16–18 NIV

Let us not become weary in doing good, for at the proper time we will reap a harvest if we do not give up.

GALATIANS 6:9 NIV

Waiting

Dear Father, it can be so hard to wait on Your timing, especially when I need rescuing from problem or pain. But Your Word says my troubles are achieving an eternal glory for me that far outweighs them all. Help me to find strength and endurance in You, believing that You use trials to mold and shape me to be more like Christ. Remind me of all the joy and blessings You provide along the way. Thank You, Father! Amen.

But you must not forget this one thing, dear friends:
A day is like a thousand years to the Lord, and a
thousand years is like a day. The Lord isn't really being
slow about his promise, as some people think. No,
he is being patient for your sake. He does not want
anyone to be destroyed, but wants everyone to repent.

2 PETER 3:8–9 NLT

"But of that day and hour no one knows,
not even the angels in heaven, nor the Son,
but only the Father. Take heed, watch and pray;
for you do not know when the time is."

MARK 13:32–33 NKJV

Teach us, O Lord, the disciplines of patience,
for to wait is often harder than to work.

PETER MARSHALL

We mistakenly look for tokens of God's
love in happiness. We should instead look
for them in His faithful and persistent
work to conform us to Christ.

JERRY BRIDGES

This letter is from Paul, a slave of God and an
apostle of Jesus Christ. I have been sent to proclaim
faith to those God has chosen and to teach them to
know the truth that shows them how to live godly lives.
This truth gives them confidence that they have eternal life,
which God—who does not lie—promised them before the
world began. And now at just the right time he has revealed
this message, which we announce to everyone.

TITUS 1:1–3 NLT

Now concerning the times and the seasons,
brothers, you have no need to have anything written
to you. For you yourselves are fully aware that the
day of the Lord will come like a thief in the night.

1 THESSALONIANS 5:1–2 ESV

Faithful Creator

We only have to glance out a window or step outside to find tangible evidence of God's amazing faithfulness. As the song goes, the "sun, moon, and stars in their courses above, join with all nature in manifold witness, to Thy great faithfulness, mercy, and love."

A stirring scripture that beautifully describes God as our faithful Creator is Isaiah 40:28–31 (NIV):

> "Do you not know?
>   Have you not heard?
> The LORD is the everlasting God,
>   the Creator of the ends of the earth.
> He will not grow tired or weary,
>   and his understanding no one can fathom.
> He gives strength to the weary
>   and increases the power of the weak.

Even youths grow tired and weary,
* and young men stumble and fall;*
but those who hope in the LORD
* will renew their strength.*
They will soar on wings like eagles;
* they will run and not grow weary,*
* they will walk and not be faint."*

The God who simply spoke not only our world but the entire universe into existence surely has the power to help us, hold us, heal us, and have mercy on us through His Son, Jesus Christ. May God's marvelous creation remind us that He is our constant hope and He is constantly faithful.

In the beginning God created
the heaven and the earth.

GENESIS 1:1 KJV

So God created man in His own image;
in the image of God He created him;
male and female He created them.

GENESIS 1:27 NKJV

The heavens are yours, and the earth is yours;
everything in the world is yours—you created it all.

PSALM 89:11 NLT

God writes the gospel not in the Bible alone,
but on trees and flowers and clouds and stars.
MARTIN LUTHER

The most universally awesome experience that
mankind knows is to stand alone on a clear
night and look at the stars. It was God who first
set the stars in space; He is their Maker and
Master. . . .such are His power and His majesty.
J. I. PACKER

All I have seen teaches me to trust
the Creator for all I have not seen.
RALPH WALDO EMERSON

*I will plant in the wilderness the cedar and the acacia
tree, the myrtle and the oil tree; I will set in the desert
the cypress tree and the pine and the box tree together,
that they may see and know, and consider and understand
together, that the hand of the LORD has done this,
and the Holy One of Israel has created it.*

ISAIAH 41:19–20 NKJV

*This is what the LORD says—your Redeemer
and Creator: "I am the LORD, who made all
things. I alone stretched out the heavens."*

ISAIAH 44:24 NLT

Childlike Wonder

Dear Father, may I always marvel at Your creation! Please help me never to lose childlike wonder over not just the vast heavens above but also a simple flower underfoot, for You have designed it all. You are a great and mighty God. Your power and artistry and glory are revealed in the majesty of Your Creation, in everything from mountains and waters to animals and people. I praise You for your awesome handiwork. You are amazing. Amen.

*Praise Him, highest heavens, and the waters that
are above the heavens! Let them praise the name of
the* LORD, *for He commanded and they were created.
He has also established them forever and ever;
He has made a decree which will not pass away.*

PSALM 148:4–6 NASB

*By faith we understand that the universe
was created by the word of God, so that what is
seen was not made out of things that are visible.*

HEBREWS 11:3 ESV

A God wise enough to create
me and the world I live in is
wise enough to watch out for me.

PHILIP YANCEY

There is a God-shaped vacuum in the heart
of every man that cannot be filled by any
created thing, but only by God, the Creator,
made known through Jesus.

BLAISE PASCAL

"To whom will you compare me? Or who is my equal?"
says the Holy One. Lift up your eyes and look to the
heavens: Who created all these? He who brings out
the starry host one by one and calls forth each of them
by name. Because of his great power and mighty
strength, not one of them is missing.

Isaiah 40:25–26 NIV

Therefore let those who suffer according to God's will
entrust their souls to a faithful Creator while doing good.

1 Peter 4:19 ESV

Not an Accident

Dear Father, it's easy to feel defeated by all the scientists and scorners who want to disprove You and Creation. But I know that this amazing earth and all the life and people You have put here are not just an accident. Like Your Word says, Your creation clearly displays You. When I am discouraged in my faith or doubting You, please forgive me and encourage me that I only need to look around at the intricate designs of the natural world to be reminded of Your reality and Your presence. Amen.

"I am the LORD; there is no other God. I have equipped you for battle, though you don't even know me, so all the world from east to west will know there is no other God. I am the LORD, and there is no other. I create the light and make the darkness. I send good times and bad times. I, the LORD, am the one who does these things."

ISAIAH 45:5–7 NLT

For we are God's handiwork, created in Christ Jesus to do good works, which God prepared in advance for us to do.

EPHESIANS 2:10 NIV

You find no difficulty in trusting the Lord
with the management of the universe and
all the outward creation, and can your
case be any more complex or difficult than
these, that you need to be anxious or
troubled about His management of it?

HANNAH WHITALL SMITH

Either we are adrift in chaos or we are
individuals, created, loved, upheld and placed
purposefully, exactly where we are. Can you
believe that? Can you trust God for that?

ELISABETH ELLIOT

For by him were all things created, that are in heaven,
and that are in earth, visible and invisible, whether
they be thrones, or dominions, or principalities,
or powers: all things were created by him, and for him.
COLOSSIANS 1:16 KJV

Put on your new nature, and be renewed as you
learn to know your Creator and become like him.
COLOSSIANS 3:10 NLT

Faithful Savior
and Peace

The "Romans Road" is a clever name for key scriptures in the book of Romans that walk us through the plan of salvation in Jesus Christ. We are all sinners and fall short of God's glory (3:23). However, although we were sinners, God showed us He loved us anyway by sending His Son to die for us (5:8). There is a steep price for our sin—*death*—but God provided the gift of Jesus Christ to cover the payment (6:23). We simply must confess with our mouths and believe in our hearts that God raised Jesus from the dead, and He is our Savior (10:9–10).

It sounds so simple; unfortunately, it's often easier said than done. When sin and pride have a stronghold in a person's life, it can be nearly impossible to let go, be humble, believe, and let God save. And there are powerful enemies working hard to keep people from salvation in Jesus (Ephesians 6:12). But those enemies

have nothing on God's power; for *nothing* is impossible with Him (Luke 1:37), *nothing* can separate us from His love (Romans 8:38–39), and *nothing* and *no one* other than Jesus Christ can save us (John 14:6; Acts 4:12).

"Pardon for sin and a peace that endureth. . ." There is no greater example of God's faithfulness to us than when He gave up His own Son to provide forgiveness for our sins and to be our Savior and our peace.

Then the angel said to them, "Do not be afraid,
for behold, I bring you good tidings of great joy which
will be to all people. For there is born to you this day
in the city of David a Savior, who is Christ the Lord.
And this will be the sign to you: You will find a Babe
wrapped in swaddling cloths, lying in a manger."

LUKE 2:10–12 NKJV

For God so loved the world, that he gave his
only begotten Son, that whosoever believeth in
him should not perish, but have everlasting life.

JOHN 3:16 KJV

The incarnation is the supreme example of
fulfilled prophecy, the supreme example
of God's faithfulness to his promises. . . .
What God did when he sent his Son into the
world is an absolute guarantee that he will do
everything he has ever promised to do.

MARTYN LLOYD-JONES

When you look at the cross, what do you see?
You see God's awesome faithfulness. Nothing—
not even the instinct to spare His own Son—
will turn him back from keeping His word.

SINCLAIR B. FERGUSON

"The LORD is my rock, my fortress and my deliverer;
my God is my rock, in whom I take refuge,
my shield and the horn of my salvation. He is
my stronghold, my refuge and my savior."

2 SAMUEL 22:2–3 NIV

You faithfully answer our prayers with awesome deeds,
O God our savior. You are the hope of everyone on earth.

PSALM 65:5 NLT

I, even I, am the LORD;
and beside me there is no saviour.

ISAIAH 43:11 KJV

Thank You for Salvation

Dear Father, it almost seems silly to say
just *thank You* for forgiving my sins, because
those two little words could never fully express
how grateful I am to You. Your Son did not
deserve the pain and shame of the cross—I
deserve that. But You gave Him up for me to
provide a way for me to come to know You.
May I never take that for granted, Lord.
You paid a huge price to save me. I owe You
everything, and I love You. Amen.

*"Now we believe, not because of what you said,
for we ourselves have heard Him and we know that
this is indeed the Christ, the Savior of the world."*

JOHN 4:42 NKJV

*We have seen and testify that the Father has sent the Son to
be the Savior of the world. Whoever confesses that Jesus is
the Son of God, God abides in him, and he in God.*

1 JOHN 4:14–15 NASB

How could God remain equally faithful to
His love for us and His just judgment of
our sins? The glory of the cross,
its unimaginable wisdom lies in the way God
has devised to provide salvation for His people.

SINCLAIR B. FERGUSON

Don't ever think that there are many ways
to the Divine. Jesus is the one qualified
mediator, the only qualified sacrifice,
and the only qualified savior.

ERWIN LUTZER

You are saved—seek to be like your Savior.

CHARLES SPURGEON

For the Lᴏʀᴅ your God is living among you.
He is a mighty savior.

Zᴇᴘᴀᴏᴛᴀᴀᴀᴠ 3:17 NLT

He has saved us and called us to a holy life—
not because of anything we have done but because of
his own purpose and grace. This grace was given us in
Christ Jesus before the beginning of time, but it has now
been revealed through the appearing of our Savior,
Christ Jesus, who has destroyed death and has brought
life and immortality to light through the gospel.

2 Tᴏᴏᴏᴏᴏ 1:9–10 NIV

Courage and Opportunity

Dear Father, I want desperately for others
to know You as Savior like I do. Why is it so
hard for me to share the Gospel at times?
I know enemies are working against me,
and my own sin gets in the way, but Your power
is so much greater than all that! Please give me
the courage and the opportunities, and use me
to show Your love and share Your Word—and
then help me trust Your Holy Spirit to work
in the lives of those around me. Amen.

*For to this end we toil and strive, because we have
our hope set on the living God, who is the Savior
of all people, especially of those who believe.*

1 TIMOTHY 4:10 ESV

*Now all glory to God, who is able to keep you from falling
away and will bring you with great joy into his glorious
presence without a single fault. All glory to him who alone
is God, our Savior through Jesus Christ our Lord.*

JUDE 24–25 NLT

*You keep him in perfect peace whose mind
is stayed on you, because he trusts in you.*

ISAIAH 26:3 ESV

Faithful Companion

Corrie ten Boom, a hero of the Christian faith during Adolf Hitler's reign of terror, endured unspeakable horrors during her time in prison and Nazi concentration camps. Her story of survival and triumph is truly miraculous. Our almighty God could have rescued her immediately from her plight, but He did not. For some people that causes doubt and anger, but for Corrie it was a God-given opportunity to share the light of Jesus in the darkest of places. That doesn't mean it wasn't awful, but Corrie knew God was constantly near. In her famous book, *The Hiding Place*, she prays, "Dear Jesus, how foolish of me to have called for human help when You are here."

Hopefully we will never have to experience anything like a Nazi concentration camp, but our lives also have their hardships, even horrors. In the midst of them, it's easy to

let ourselves believe God has abandoned us.
Despite how we *feel* about what we're trying to
endure, we must *choose* to trust God's promises,
just like Corrie ten Boom did. We must cling
to His Word to sustain us. And He has said,
"Never will I leave you; never will I forsake you"
(Hebrews 13:5 NIV).

Though we cannot understand all His ways,
God is always with us; He is our most faithful
companion. We never need to feel alone, and
we can gratefully sing to Him our praises for
His "dear presence to cheer and to guide."

He tends his flock like a shepherd: He gathers the lambs in his arms and carries them close to his heart; he gently leads those that have young.

ISAIAH 40:11 NIV

Fear not, for I am with you; be not dismayed, for I am your God.

ISAIAH 41:10 ESV

Because God is with you all the time,
no place is any closer to God than
the place where you are right now.

RICK WARREN

God cannot give us a happiness and
peace apart from Himself, because it
is not there. There is no such thing.

C. S. LEWIS

Nevertheless I am continually with You;
You have taken hold of my right hand.

PSALM 73:23 NASB

"And I will ask the Father, and he will give you
another Helper, to be with you forever, even the
Spirit of truth, whom the world cannot receive,
because it neither sees him nor knows him. You know
him, for he dwells with you and will be in you."

JOHN 14:16–17 ESV

Never without You

Dear Father, I don't know what I would do or
where I would be without You. I'm so thankful
I never have to walk a single road or go through
any season of life alone. I need Your guidance
and presence so much. You are constantly with
me and know my every move and every thought.
Knowing this, I want to please You and draw
closer to You in all that I do. Amen.

"Remain in me, and I will remain in you. For a branch cannot produce fruit if it is severed from the vine, and you cannot be fruitful unless you remain in me."

JOHN 15:4 NLT

Submit yourselves therefore to God. Resist the devil, and he will flee from you. Draw near to God, and he will draw near to you.

JAMES 4:7–8 ESV

Frequently remind yourself that God is
with you, that He will never fail you,
that you can count upon Him. Say these
words, "God is with me, helping me."
NORMAN VINCENT PEALE

Do not limit the limitless God!
With Him, face the future unafraid
because you are never alone.
MRS. CHARLES E. COWMAN

For it is God who is at work in you, both
to will and to work for His good pleasure.
PHILIPPIANS 2:13 NASB

What you have learned and received and
heard and seen in me—practice these things,
and the God of peace will be with you.
PHILIPPIANS 4:9 ESV

And, lo, I am with you always,
even unto the end of the world.
MATTHEW 28:20 KJV

Extra Reassurance

Dear Father, sometimes I wish I could feel Your presence more tangibly. I wish I could literally dial a number to heaven and talk with You on the phone or invite You to sit on my couch and chat. And when I am hurting, sometimes I desperately want to feel Your strong, loving arms around me. At those times, please remind me of Your presence in other ways, through Your people and Your Word and Your Holy Spirit in me. I do know You are here; sometimes I just need extra reassurance. Amen.

*Whoever keeps his commandments abides in God,
and God in him. And by this we know that he
abides in us, by the Spirit whom he has given us.*

1 JOHN 3:24 ESV

*But you belong to God, my dear children. You have already
won a victory over those people, because the Spirit who
lives in you is greater than the spirit who lives in the world.*

1 JOHN 4:4 NLT

Faithful Encourager
and Guide

God's Word tells us many times to encourage
each other in our faith, and we must strive to
do so daily (Hebrews 3:13). But too often we
fail each other. Not one of us is perfect; we will
let down others who need encouragement, and
we will be let down, too. That shouldn't stop
us from trying, however; and thankfully God is
a faithful encourager (Romans 15:5) who *never*
fails us. When we are discouraged, the simple
act of reading His Word and meditating on His
promises has dramatic power to lift us up out of
the deepest despair.

His Word is also a lamp for our feet and a
light for our path (Psalm 119:105). Through
His Word, He is our faithful Guide on every
road of life, whether it's smooth, broad, and
easy—or rocky, narrow, and hard. In every
season and every circumstance, we can count
on God to go before us and show us the way.

But He won't force us to follow Him. We can choose to find our own way—or we can choose to ask directions from the sovereign, all-knowing God who created everything and loves us more than anything. Obviously the latter is the wiser.

"Thine own dear presence to cheer and to guide. . ." Our God knows us; He is rooting for us; He knows the best way for us. How blessed we are to never have to go it alone!

*May the God of endurance and encouragement grant
you to live in such harmony with one another, in accord
with Christ Jesus, that together you may with one voice
glorify the God and Father of our Lord Jesus Christ.*

ROMANS 15:5–6 ESV

*As soon as I pray, you answer me;
you encourage me by giving me strength.*

PSALM 138:3 NLT

Encouragement is
the oxygen of the soul.
JOHN MAXWELL

I wonder how many believers today realize that
faith is not merely believing that Christ died
for our sins. Faith is also being confident that
His way is better than sin. His will is more
wise. His help is more sure. His promises more
precious. And His reward more satisfying. Faith
begins with a backward look at the cross, but it
lives with a forward look at the promises.
JOHN PIPER

*You, L*ORD*, hear the desire of the afflicted;*
you encourage them, and you listen to their cry.

PSALM 10:17 NIV

Is there any encouragement from belonging to Christ?
Any comfort from his love? Any fellowship together
in the Spirit? Are your hearts tender and compassionate?
Then make me truly happy by agreeing wholeheartedly
with each other, loving one another, and working
together with one mind and purpose.

PHILIPPIANS 2:1–3 NLT

When I'm Feeling Down

Dear Father, just watching the news is
enough to get me totally discouraged,
and sometimes when I'm feeling down it's
hard to get back up. Family and friends
can only do so much, but You encourage
unfailingly. Please help me cling to the
promises of Your Word, call out to You in
constant prayer, and remember the presence
of Your Holy Spirit to encourage
and guide me. Amen.

The humble will see their God at work and be glad.
Let all who seek God's help be encouraged.
For the LORD hears the cries of the needy.

PSALM 69:32–33 NLT

I weep with sorrow; encourage me by your word.

PSALM 119:28 NLT

We aren't just thrown on this earth
like dice tossed across a table. We are
lovingly placed here for a purpose.

CHARLES SWINDOLL

Discipleship is a daily discipline; we follow
Jesus a step at a time, a day at a time.

WARREN WIERSBE

No matter how steep the mountain—
the Lord is going to climb it with you.

HELEN STEINER RICE

*Show me Your ways, O LORD; teach me
Your paths. Lead me in Your truth and teach
me, for You are the God of my salvation.*

PSALM 25:4–5 NKJV

*Trust in the LORD with all thine heart; and lean
not unto thine own understanding. In all thy ways
acknowledge him, and he shall direct thy paths.*

PROVERBS 3:5–6 KJV

Love for Your Word

Dear Father, please give me the desire, ability, and persistence to memorize Your Word. It truly is a lamp for my feet and a light to my path. I need to not simply read it; I need to be able to recall it from memory, so that no matter the circumstance I'm equipped with Truth to face it. Your Word is my guide. Help me not to take it for granted but to memorize it, treasure it, and apply it. Amen.

You guide me with your counsel,
leading me to a glorious destiny.

PSALM 73:24 NLT

Teach me to do Your will, for You are my God;
let Your good Spirit lead me on level ground.

PSALM 143:10 NASB

The heart of man plans his way,
but the Lord establishes his steps.

PROVERBS 16:9 ESV

Faithful Strength

An Old Testament name synonymous with the word *strength* is Samson. He was an ancient-times Mr. Incredible, able to do things like tear apart an attacking lion with his bare hands (Judges 14:4–6) and fight off an army of a thousand men with the jawbone of a donkey (Judges 15:15–17). But his strength was not without conditions, and its secret was in his long locks of hair; his parents had promised God before his birth that it would never be cut. But then he met a woman named Delilah. . . .

While there are plenty of strong and physically fit people in the world, there are no modern-day Samsons or Mr. Incredibles, and even the strongest person cannot maintain strength forever. Our bodies age and deteriorate, for we are, in fact, merely human.

Thankfully God's strength has no conditions or limits. It can be trusted completely. He alone

is our faithful Strength. We can confidently say, "My flesh and my heart may fail, but God is the strength of my heart and my portion forever" (Psalm 73:26 NIV).

As the song goes, He provides "strength for today" physically, emotionally, and spiritually, to face any and every challenge we might come up against—and not just today but *every* day.

God is our refuge and strength,
a very present help in trouble.

PSALM 46:1 KJV

But You, O LORD, do not be far from Me;
O My Strength, hasten to help Me!

PSALM 22:19 NKJV

I will strengthen you and help you.
I will hold you up with my victorious right hand.

ISAIAH 41:10 NLT

We can be tired, weary, and emotionally distraught, but after spending time alone with God, we find that He injects into our bodies energy, power, and strength.

CHARLES STANLEY

Now what greater comfort is there than this, that there is one who presides in the world who is so wise he cannot be mistaken, so faithful he cannot deceive, so pitiful he cannot neglect his people, and so powerful that he can make stones even to be turned into bread if he please!

STEPHEN CHARNOCK

The Sovereign LORD is my strength; he makes my feet like the feet of a deer, he enables me to tread on the heights.

HABAKKUK 3:19 NIV

Hear my cry, O God, listen to my prayer; from the end of the earth I call to you when my heart is faint. Lead me to the rock that is higher than I, for you have been my refuge, a strong tower against the enemy.

PSALM 61:1–3 ESV

Delighting in Weakness

Dear Father, my human strength is nothing
compared to Your great strength, and only
when I delight in my weakness will I truly realize
how strong You are. But my pride doesn't
easily delight in weakness. I like to be able to do
things on my own. Please humble me and make
me weak so that You can be strong in me and
I can give all the glory to You. Amen.

"My grace is all you need. My power works best in weakness." So now I am glad to boast about my weaknesses, so that the power of Christ can work through me. That's why I take pleasure in my weaknesses, and in the insults, hardships, persecutions, and troubles that I suffer for Christ. For when I am weak, then I am strong.

2 CORINTHIANS 12:9–10 NLT

For I can do everything through Christ, who gives me strength.

PHILIPPIANS 4:13 NLT

My attitude was and still is like that of
David, who was ashamed that the armies
of Israel would tremble before Goliath.
Without hesitation he stepped forward with
complete confidence in the God who had
proven Himself to be faithful (1 Samuel 17).
For David, the size of the giant was irrelevant.

DAVE HUNT

The assurance of the believer is not that
God will save him even if he stops believing,
but that God will keep him believing—
God will sustain you in faith, he will make
your hope firm and stable to the end.
He will cause you to persevere.

JOHN PIPER

The Lᴏʀᴅ is my strength and my shield; my heart trusted in
Him, and I am helped; therefore my heart greatly rejoices,
and with my song I will praise Him. The Lᴏʀᴅ is their
strength, and He is the saving refuge of His anointed.

Psalm 28:7–8 nkjv

"Behold, God is my salvation, I will trust and
not be afraid; for the Lᴏʀᴅ Gᴏᴅ is my strength
and song, and He has become my salvation."

Isaiah 12:2 nasb

You Sustain Me

Dear Father, I have experienced times in my life
when nothing has been holding me up except
You. Thank You for being my strength. I know
times like that will come again, and though my
first reaction is to fear and dread them, I need
to remember how You have sustained me in
the past. Nothing is coming my way that You
and I can't handle together. Please give me
confidence in Your strength, in Your power,
and in Your love for me. Amen.

Search for the LORD and for his strength; continually seek him. Remember the wonders he has performed, his miracles, and the rulings he has given.
PSALM 105:4–5 NLT

LORD, be gracious to us; we long for you. Be our strength every morning, our salvation in time of distress.
ISAIAH 33:2 NIV

Be strong in the Lord, and in the power of his might.
EPHESIAN 6:10 KJV

Faithful Hope

Chuck Colson was an adviser to President Richard Nixon from 1969 to 1973, was deeply involved in the Watergate scandal, and was sentenced to federal prison for obstruction of justice. You'd think a man brought down from power like that would lose all hope—and he did lose hope in himself and in politics and in this world. But he found real and lasting hope in Jesus Christ. He became a Christian in 1973, and in 1974 he served seven months in prison. He was released with a new mission to start a prison ministry, which resulted in Prison Fellowship, the largest outreach to prisoners, ex-prisoners, and their families.

Colson said once in a famous speech, "Where is the hope? I meet millions of people that tell me that they feel demoralized by the decay around us. Where is the hope? The hope that each of us has is not in who governs us, or

what laws are passed, or what great things we
do as a nation. Our hope is in the power of
God working through the hearts of people.
That's where our hope lies in this country.
And that's where our hope lies in our life."

We are often part of the millions Colson
refers to who feel demoralized by decay. And if
we put our hope in anything other than God's
power working through people, which He
does through salvation in Jesus Christ, we will
always end up defeated. He is our "bright hope
for tomorrow," our faithful and lasting hope.
Where is the hope, we ask? The answer is always
in God our Father and our Savior Jesus Christ.

Why am I discouraged? Why is my heart so sad?
I will put my hope in God! I will praise him
again—my Savior and my God!

PSALM 42:5–6 NLT

For I know the thoughts that I think toward you,
says the LORD, thoughts of peace and not of evil,
to give you a future and a hope.

JEREMIAH 29:11 NKJV

We should ask God to increase our hope when it is small, awaken it when it is dormant, confirm it when it is wavering, strengthen it when it is weak, and raise it up when it is overthrown.

JOHN CALVIN

God is more interested in your future and your relationships than you are.

BILLY GRAHAM

Rejoice in hope, be patient in tribulation,
be constant in prayer.

ROMANS 12:12 ESV

May the God of hope fill you with all joy and peace
as you trust in him, so that you may overflow
with hope by the power of the Holy Spirit.

ROMANS 15:13 NIV

The Scriptures give us hope and encouragement as
we wait patiently for God's promises to be fulfilled.

ROMANS 15:4 NLT

Our Only Hope

Dear Father, we live in such a hurting world.
I don't know how anyone falls asleep at night
without believing in Your Word and that
You are sovereign and in control. I cannot
understand all Your ways, and I have so many
questions. But ultimately I know that You are
our only hope, and You will make all things
right one day. Help me to keep trusting in
Your promises, and help me to share Your
love and Your truth so that others will find
the only true hope in You, too. Amen.

Having been justified by faith, we have peace with God through our Lord Jesus Christ, through whom also we have access by faith into this grace in which we stand, and rejoice in hope of the glory of God. And not only that, but we also glory in tribulations, knowing that tribulation produces perseverance; and perseverance, character; and character, hope. Now hope does not disappoint, because the love of God has been poured out in our hearts by the Holy Spirit who was given to us.

ROMANS 5:1–5 NKJV

I have held many things in my hands,
and I have lost them all; but whatever I have
placed in God's hands, that I still possess.

MARTIN LUTHER

God is the only one who can make
the valley of trouble a door of hope.

CATHERINE MARSHALL

If in this life only we have hope in Christ,
we are of all men most miserable.

1 CORINTHIANS 15:19 KJV

Praise be to the God and Father of our Lord Jesus Christ!
In his great mercy he has given us new birth into a living
hope through the resurrection of Jesus Christ from the
dead, and into an inheritance that can never perish, spoil
or fade. This inheritance is kept in heaven for you.

1 PETER 1:3–4 NIV

Pressing On

Dear Father, even though I ultimately trust in You, in the midst of a discouraging situation, there are days I let my emotions rule and I go around acting hopeless. Forgive me and keep me pressing on, confident that this world is not all there is. Please give me joy on the journey and help me to remember that my hope is in You and my home is in heaven. Amen.

Be strong and take heart,
all you who hope in the LORD.

PSALM 31:24 NIV

For You are my hope, O Lord GOD;
you are my trust from my youth.
By You I have been upheld from birth.

PSALM 71:5–6 NKJV

Faithfully Worthy

"Great is Thy faithfulness, Great is Thy faithfulness. . .Great is Thy Faithfulness, Lord unto me." In the chorus of this beautiful hymn, we sing over and over of God's great faithfulness. He deserves our worship again and again—and again. He deserves it because He is always Sovereign, always Creator, always King of kings, always Lord of lords; yet He is also always our loving, everlasting Father whom we can call Abba and who never makes a mistake. He is faithfully unchanging, compassionate, amazing, and merciful. He faithfully provides for us and keeps time for us. He is our Savior, Encourager, and Guide. He is our faithful Strength, Hope, and Peace. For all of those reasons and many more, He is faithfully worthy of all our praise.

Revelation 4:8 (NLT) gives an extraordinary word picture of worship to God, describing

living creatures who surround His throne day and night and who never stop singing these praises to Him: "Holy, holy, holy is the Lord God, the Almighty—the one who always was, who is, and who is still to come."

As we go about the number of days we've been given, with our faithful God guiding and helping us, may we not only praise Him with song but strive to make our every thought and deed an act of worship to the only One who is *always* worthy.

*Make a joyful noise to the L*ORD*, all the earth! Serve the L*ORD *with gladness! Come into his presence with singing! Know that the L*ORD*, he is God! It is he who made us, and we are his; we are his people, and the sheep of his pasture. Enter his gates with thanksgiving, and his courts with praise! Give thanks to him; bless his name! For the L*ORD *is good; his steadfast love endures forever, and his faithfulness to all generations.*

PSALM 100 ESV

Words Aren't Enough

Dear Father, no words can fully describe how in awe I am of You and how grateful I am that You love me. I bow before You in worship for all that You are and all that You do. You know my heart, and You know I love You. But my words and thoughts and songs are not nearly enough to praise You. Please help me make everything I do an act of love and worship to You, in a way that others will want to praise You, too! Amen.

Praise ye the LORD. Praise God in his sanctuary:
praise him in the firmament of his power.
Praise him for his mighty acts:
praise him according to his excellent greatness.
Praise him with the sound of the trumpet:
praise him with the psaltery and harp.
Praise him with the timbrel and dance:
praise him with stringed instruments and organs.
Praise him upon the loud cymbals:
praise him upon the high sounding cymbals.
Let every thing that hath breath praise the LORD.
Praise ye the LORD.

PSALM 150 KJV

God wills to be displayed and known and
loved and cherished and worshipped.

JOHN PIPER

It is in the process of being worshipped that
God communicates His presence to men.

C. S. LEWIS

The more you praise God, the more you
become God-conscious and absorbed in His
greatness, wisdom, faithfulness, and love.
Praise reminds you of all that God is able to do
and of great things He has already done.

WESLEY L. DUEWEL

*Ascribe to the L<small>ORD</small> the glory due to
His name; worship the L<small>ORD</small> in holy array.*

P<small>SALM</small> 29:2 <small>NASB</small>

*While Jesus was here on earth, he offered prayers
and pleadings, with a loud cry and tears, to the one
who could rescue him from death. And God heard his
prayers because of his deep reverence for God.*

H<small>EBREWS</small> 5:7 <small>NLT</small>

My All in All

Dear Father, forgive me that too often I'm just giving you lip service and not wholehearted worship, like when I'm distracted during the music at church and when I'm too flippant about You and Your Word. I want to fully revere You for who You are because You absolutely deserve it. I want You to be my all in all. Help me to draw closer to You and worship You with everything You've given me. Amen.

And so, dear brothers and sisters, I plead with you to give your bodies to God because of all he has done for you. Let them be a living and holy sacrifice—the kind he will find acceptable. This is truly the way to worship him.

ROMANS 12:1 NLT